KT-162-097

USING THIS BOOK

Children learn to read by reading, but they need help to begin with.

When you have read the story on the left-hand pages aloud to the child, go back to the beginning of the book and look at the pictures together.

Encourage children to read the sentences under the pictures. If they don't know a word, give them a chance to 'guess' what it is from the illustrations, before telling them.

There are more suggestions for helping children to learn to read in the *Parent/Teacher* booklet.

British Library Cataloguing in Publication Data

McCullagh, Sheila K.
   Old Mr. Gotobed. —(Puddle Lane. Series. no.
   855; stage 3, v. 1)
   I. Title   II. Dillow, John,   III. Series
   428.6   PR6063.A165/
   ISBN 0-7214-0934-2

First edition

© Text and layout SHEILA McCULLAGH MCMLXXXV
© In publication LADYBIRD BOOKS LTD MCMLXXXV

Old Mr Gotobed

written by SHEILA McCULLAGH
illustrated by JOHN DILLOW

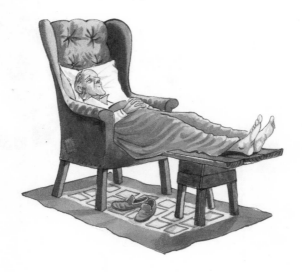

This book belongs to:

_____

Ladybird Books Loughborough

Old Mr Gotobed lived in Puddle Lane.
He lived in a house at the end.
The house had a roof
made of red-brown tiles.

Old Mr Gotobed
lived in Puddle Lane.

One night, it began to rain.
It rained and it rained and
it rained, until all
the puddles in Puddle Lane
were full of water.

Then the wind began to blow.
The wind blew and it blew
and it **blew**,
and it whistled round the houses
in Puddle Lane.

It rained and
it rained
in Puddle Lane.
The wind blew
and it blew
and it blew.

7

The wind blew harder and harder.
It blew under the tiles
on the roof of Mr Gotobed's house.
It blew some of the tiles
off the roof, and down
into the lane.

There was a hole in the roof,
where the tiles had been.

The rain ran down the roof.
It ran down into the hole.
It came in through the hole,
and dripped on to the floor
of the attic.
Drip, drip, drip.

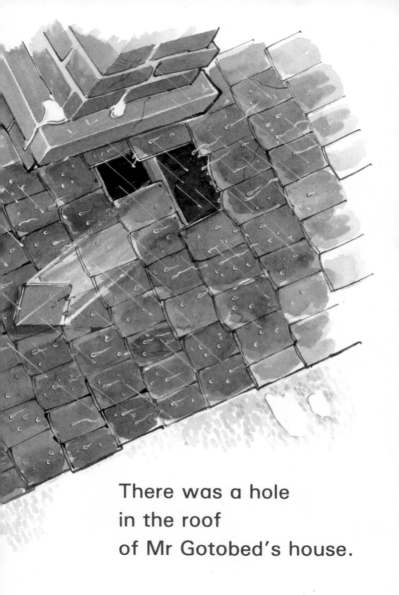

There was a hole
in the roof
of Mr Gotobed's house.

At seven o'clock in the morning,
old Mr Gotobed got up.
The rain was still raining,
and the wind was still blowing.
So he didn't go out,
and he didn't see the hole
in the roof.

Old Mr Gotobed
got up at seven o'clock.

At eight o'clock, old Mr Gotobed
had his breakfast.
The rain was still raining
and the wind was still blowing.
Old Mr Gotobed still didn't go out,
so he didn't see the hole
in the roof.

Old Mr Gotobed
had breakfast
at eight o'clock.

Old Mr Gotobed had dinner at eleven.
(He always felt hungry in the morning.)
The rain was still raining,
and the wind was still blowing.
Old Mr Gotobed still didn't go out,
so he still didn't see the hole
in the roof.

Old Mr Gotobed
had dinner
at eleven o'clock.

An hour later, the clock struck twelve.
It was noon.
Old Mr Gotobed looked out
of the window.
The rain was still raining,
and the wind was still blowing.
"There's no place like bed,
when it's wet and it's windy,"
said old Mr Gotobed.
And he went back to bed.

Old Mr Gotobed
went to bed at noon.

Mr Gotobed was fast asleep
when, at last, the rain stopped.
Up in the attic of Mr Gotobed's house,
there was a very big puddle.
The rain had been coming in all day.

There was
a very big puddle
in the attic.

The wind blew the clouds away.
But the very big puddle
was still there in the attic.
It was just over Mr Gotobed's bed.

Three drops of water dripped
through a crack in the ceiling.
They dripped on to Mr Gotobed's toes.

Plop! Plop! Plop!

But Mr Gotobed went on sleeping.

The water dripped
on to Mr Gotobed's toes.
Plop! Plop! Plop!

The water ran along the crack
in the ceiling.
Three drops of water dripped
on to Mr Gotobed's knees.

Plop! Plop! Plop!

But Mr Gotobed went on sleeping.

The water dripped
on to Mr Gotobed's knees.
Plop! Plop! Plop!

The moon came up
over the roofs of the houses
in Puddle Lane.
The clouds had all blown away.
But the water was still running
along the crack in the ceiling.
Three drops of water dripped
on to Mr Gotobed's nose.

Plop! Plop! Plop!

The water dripped
on to Mr Gotobed's nose.
Plop! Plop! Plop!

Mr Gotobed woke up.

He saw the moon shining
in at the window.
He was just going to get up,
when the water in the attic
reached a hole in the ceiling.
All the water that was left
in the attic fell through
on to Mr Gotobed's head
in one big swoosh!

The water fell
on to Mr Gotobed's head –
swoosh!

Poor Mr Gotobed!
He was **very** wet.
He got out of bed, and
put on some warm, dry clothes.
Then he climbed up a ladder
into the attic, and saw
the hole in the roof.

Mr Gotobed saw
the hole in the roof.

Mr Gotobed shook his head.
"Oh dear! Oh dear!"
said Mr Gotobed.
There was an old tin bath
in the roof.
Mr Gotobed pulled the bath
under the hole.

Mr Gotobed pulled
the tin bath
under the hole.

He climbed back down the ladder,
and looked at his bed.
His bed was **very** wet.

Mr Gotobed went downstairs.
He made up a bed by the fire.

By the time the moon
was high in the sky,
and shining down into the lane,
old Mr Gotobed
was all tucked in,
asleep in bed again.

And when the moon
shone down in the lane,
old Mr Gotobed
went to bed again.

Parent/teacher please note:

On the following pages the whole story of Old Mr Gotobed is retold in rhyme. Read the rhyme on the opposite page aloud to the child first.

From page 36, Mr Gotobed's rhyme is repeated for the child to read with illustrations to help him.* Talk about the pictures and encourage him to read the words underneath.

*It doesn't matter that the child may be **reading** partly from memory. He is still learning to read and learning incidentally that words which end in the same sound often (but not always) end in the same combination of letters.*

**Footnote:* In order to avoid the continual "he or she", "him or her", the child is referred to in this book as "he". However, the stories are equally appropriate to girls and boys.

34

When the Magician who lived in the old
house at the end of Puddle Lane heard
about Mr Gotobed,
he turned the story
into a rhyme.
Here is the rhyme:

Old Mr Gotobed
gets up at seven.
His breakfast is
at eight o'clock,
his dinner at eleven.
Old Mr Gotobed
goes to bed at noon.
He doesn't get up
till he sees the moon.
And when the moon
shines down in the lane,
old Mr Gotobed
goes to bed again.

Old Mr Gotobed
gets up at seven.

His breakfast is
at eight o'clock,
his dinner at eleven.

Old Mr Gotobed
goes to bed at noon.

He doesn't get up
till he sees the moon.

And when the moon
shines down in the lane,

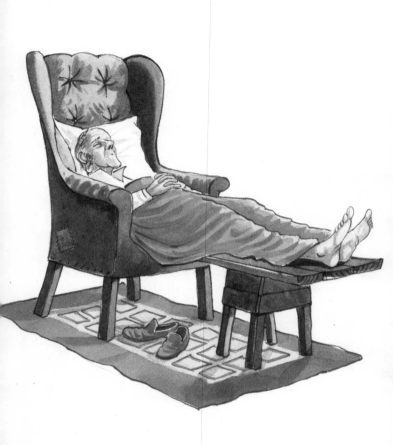

old Mr Gotobed
goes to bed again.

Notes for the parent/teacher

When you have read the story, go back to the beginning. Look at each picture and talk about it, pointing to the caption below, and reading it aloud yourself.

Run your finger along under the words as you read, so that the child learns that reading goes from left to right. (You needn't say this in so many words. Children learn many useful things about reading by just reading with you, and it is often better to let them learn by experience, rather than by explanation.) When you next go through the book, encourage the child to read the words and sentences under the illustrations.

Mrs Pitter-Patter dropped the tail with a yell. She made such a noise, that she woke Mr Gotobed, who was fast asleep in bed in the house at the end of the lane.

Mr Gotobed woke up.

Don't rush in with the word before he* has time to think, but don't leave him struggling for too long. Always encourage him to feel that he is reading successfully, praising him when he does well, and avoiding criticism.

Now turn back to the beginning, and print the child's name in the space on the title page, using ordinary, not capital letters. Let him watch you print it: this is another useful experience.

Children enjoy hearing the same story many times. Read this one as often as the child likes hearing it. The more opportunities he has of looking at the illustrations and **reading** the captions with you, the more he will come to recognise the words. Don't worry if he **remembers** rather than **reads** the captions. This is a normal stage in learning.

If you have a number of books, let him choose which story he would like to have again.

Footnote: In order to avoid the continual "he or she", "him or her", the child is referred to in this book as "he". However, the stories are equally appropriate to girls and boys.

All the books at each Stage are separate stories and are written at the same reading level. It is important for children to read as many books as possible at each Stage before going on to the next Stage.

Here are more stories about the characters in Puddle Lane:

Stage 3

2 **Hickory Mouse**
In this story the Wideawake Mice meet Hickory and you can find out what happens when he dances on top of the clock.

3 **The Gruffle in Puddle Lane**
This is a story about a monster who can vanish when he wants to.

Hickory Mouse